Bohemian Rhythms

A collection of poems

Urvashi Ray Tongia

First Published in March 2023

ISBN: 978-93-5741-317-6

BLUEROSE PUBLISHERS

www.BlueRoseONE.com

info@bluerosepublishers.com

+91 8882 898 898

Cover Design:

Muskan Sachdeva

Typographic Design:

Hemlata

Distributed by: BlueRose, Amazon, Flipkart

The book is dedicated to my late mom
"Sanghamitra"

"The hand that rocks the cradle, rules the world!!"

About The Book

What is Poetry exactly?

William Wordsworth: Poetry is the spontaneous overflow of powerful feelings!!

Robert Frost: Poetry is when emotion has found its thoughts and the thought has found words!!

Urvashi Ray Tongia: Poetry echoes deep sentiments of my heart!!

Bohemian Rhythms has touched everything under the sun!! Be it nature, sports, humans, personal issues, social causes, politics, gender issues, Covid!!

Its a juxtaposition of sorts!!

If its serious heavy duty stuff, its lighthearted to read as well!!

The poet speaks straight from the heart and calls a spade a spade, without sounding controversial!!

The tete a tetes, the day to day affairs, seen through a poet"s eyes or explored deeply have been given the form of verses, as they say:

"A pen is mightier than the Sword"

Acknowledgements

Growing up in an amiable environment and having umpteen coffee table conversations with friends, bought my creativity alive!!

Deeply indebted to my Dad, my friend, philosopher and guide for always egging me on to grow big as a writer!!

Dad, with your blessings, i"ve finally got my book published!!

Heartfelt thanks to my lovely daughter pihu and my sister Sunanda for their unconditional love and support

Last but not the least, i would like to thank my husband Sumit and my inlaws Santosh and Suman who were with me throughout this journey of life!!

Contents

Gossipmongers.. 1

Catfish... 2

The rape victim 3

Anonymous 4

On the rebound.. 5

The hand that rocks the cradle.................................... 6

Waka Waka.. 7

Cancer 8

The Tinder Swindler 9

Mutilated 10

The diary of a suicide bomber 11

The fitness freak... 12

Hounded by Publishers 13

Sour Grapes.. 14

A poem dedicated to Adidev on his birthday 15

Whispers in the Corridor.. 16

Fan... 17

Vacation 18

Dusshera 19

Nepotism.. 20

Flowers in the graveyard.. 21

Weather blues... 22

The Teacher.. 23

Junk food.. 24

Books 25

Special Child 26

Cassanova 28

India, My Motherland!! 29

Honeytrap 30

Solitude 32

Why i write 33

The birthday girl 34

Hypocrisy 35

Ode to a single mother 37

The martyr 39

Status Symbol 41

The beggar 43

Recluse 45

Clickbait 46

Vendetta 47

Depression 48

Beyond Bhubaneshwar 49

Aarav....The rockstar 50

Ode to a father 52

Superstition 53

Summertime 55

Hope 56

Fashion Show 57

Narcissist 58

Reunion 59

Rendezvous 60

Golddigger 61

Rhythm of the Rain 62

Netflix 63

Kleptomaniac 64

Morning Walk...65

Modern Love 66

The courier guy!!..67

The IPL fever 68

Creativity..69

KK..70

Dreams and Despair...71

Childhood..72

Harakari of the English language............................73

Who am I??...74

Doppleganger!..75

Accident 76

Daydreaming 77

Emotions..78

#Me Too...79

Gossipmongers

The women gathered under one roof
To gather some more spoof
Of scandals emanating as proof
To ensure a front page scoop!!

Rolling eyes focused,chewing beetle leaf
Layers of pancake as a shield
The neighbourhood aunt shook her bead
What a spirited day its indeed!!

Lost to the world,the tete a tete was on
The escapades of the glamorous diva to catch on
The paramour she apparently vanished with to reckon
Such a matter of priority was discussed spot on

The shouts grew by the dozen
And she remained frozen
While she was busy being a snoopy intruder
The apple of her eyes had eloped with her lover!!

Catfish

She mistook him for her Prince Charming!!
He fell for her charms hook,line and sinker
Opposites attracted,lured by the fantasy
A picture perfect partner awaits me,
Their die hard focus was on social media

Assuming the identity of an unknown
Duping and defrauding was their sole aim
Waiting to turn into Cinderalla, she swayed
While he serenaded as Romeo under her window!!

Unbecknownst to the other,both were laying a trap
Who was the victim here,who the perperator
Living in a world of make believe, her hopes came crashing
He was a pauper, and she a Catfish!!

The rape victim

Her dignity torn to shreds,
She lay weeping in the courtroom
As if the act of violence wasnt enough
Her chastity and length of attire was under attack!!

Was i really raped by the aggressor,she pondered
Or my rape is happening here in court of justice!!
The society will never forgive you mindwell!!
The victim has to counter more pain than the perpetrator!!

Labelled a slut,called a woman of questionable character!!
Her cries for help had gone unnoticed by the bystanders!!
Parents were more interested in her prospect in the
marriage market
If word gets out about "the incident"!!

No wonder women don"t come forward!!
Once a victim of rape,remains forever a victim of rape
I'm not the guilty one,she says,you all are!!
Since i can"t take law into my own hands
She jumps to her death,to escape being raped again!!

Anonymous

I prefer to remain anonymous!!
Why??
Some shout from the rooftops
Others reap benefits through paid media
I believe in keeping a low profile

Won"t that cost you big time?
No one is aware of your good deeds
If you don"t reveal your identity
End up being a non entity!!

My aim is not to please all
Its also not about winning friends and influencing people
I prefer the shadow of darkness to the sunshine of glory
Being solo gives me happiness,not worry!!

Left to my own devices I can create my destiny
Without letting anybody dictate terms
Nameless,faceless i can be a fighter
A survivor belittling all odds!!

Happy living in a state of anonymity
Ensured a state of depravity
Nobody knew what happened to her
By the time anybody reached out,she ended up as a
charity!!!

On the rebound

Catching up with an old flame,
She tried to revive the memories again
Time went ticking by
The whirlwind romance was about to die

The clandestine meet ups,far from the prying eyes
Seemed adventurous, a moment to defy
Prancing around like newly weds, they felt
The heart skipped beats in their love nest!!

When the initial heat of the romance collapsed
Cooling their heels,they were left aghast
The very passionate encounters they had cherised
Turned their ecstacies into agonies released!!

He was a changed man,so was she
Whom are we fooling,certainly not me!!
Speaking to herself,she did a U turn
Back at her abode,never to return!!

The hand that rocks the cradle

An all giving entity,she"s a woman of substance
Staying awake till the wee hours
Keeping duty before beauty
A pure and giving soul!!

Being omnipresent everywhere
Yes,she can multitask
Completing her deadline along with household chores
Running around from pillar to post!!

Sacrifice is just another word
Added to her dictionary
Stifling a yawn,with a smile on face
Going on and about on toes from dusk until dawn!!

Where does all this energy come from??
We wonder,yes,its something to ponder!!
Its remarkable,its creditable indeed
The hand that rocks the cradle can rule the world!!

Waka Waka

As the countdown to worldcup begins
Im sure the palpitations reach the zenith
The fans pray that their country wins
The hooligans eager to go wild from within

Neither is Shakira there to perform Waka Waka to
cheer Pique
Nor is there alcohol to trigger the burning spirits
Yet,the die hard soccer addicts are on their way
To motivate their nation,their pride heresay!!

As Qatar plays the opening match as hosts
Im sure there will be plenty of encouraging posts
Social Media is full of trolls
It ensures we are on a roll

Cancer

Such a deadly disease
To escape from its clutches is a miracle indeed
I salute all the cancer survivors
Its a feat not everyone achieves

Follow a healthy lifestyle they say
Only then will you be able to keep it at bay
There"s no scientific explanation i pray
Ive seen disciplined aged and young fall prey

Don"t neglect if ever there is a sign
An early treatment might ensure you are fine
It can be treated and cured at an early stage
The more you neglect,the less you leave to fate!!

The Tinder Swindler

He proclaimed to be God"s greatest gift to women
They fell prey to his delirious charms easily
Swiping left,right and centre
They gave the don juan easy access to their domain!!

Luring and duping helpless women
He left them bereft of their money
Breaking their heart in the process
He moved on to the next target!!

His jet set lifestyle combined with Greek God looks,
Attracted ladies like bees to honey
Till they figured out what had struck them
They had been swindled out of their fortune!!

We call women gold diggers but forget cassanovas
Love them and leave them as his prime motive
Beware!! The Tinder Swindler is on a prowl!!

Mutilated

Leaving her birth abode
She stepped into a new one
Hoping the scent of love
Will ensure her beautiful living

Initial months went by peacefully
Instagram,twitter,facebook and snapchat
Depicted a picture perfect existence!!

A twist in the tale was about to enfold
The social media account was put on hold
Life was not as rosy,was never meant to be

Severing ties from the family cost her big time
The farce of living in was exposed in a while
Love had flown out of the window soon enough
The corpse was found mutilated and chopped beyond
recognition!!

The diary of a suicide bomber

Losing the zest to live,a putty in the hands of the terrorists
The suicide bombers went around doing their duty
We have a mission to upkeep
No time to sit and weep!!

Was it by choice,the co conspirators were asked!!
When post release they expressed their repentance
and grief
Breathing in the fresh air of relief
All they could say was peace!!

That time we had the leaders to appease
Losing our sanity was indeed the need
Coming to terms with it,as reality sunk in
All we could do was cry from within

The fitness freak

He sweat it out in the gym profusely
The fitness fanatic in him aiming at a target
I have to get my 6 or 8 pack abs
Working out and burning calories is the mantra!!

Thriving on protein shakes and bars
He went out and about like a maniac
The thirst for achieving a perfect body
Converting flab into fab was his hobby!!

The treadmill kept on rocking to and fro
Collapsing happened at one go!!
Aiming to be the man about town
His body was found lost and down!!

Hounded by Publishers

An aspiring poet and novelist
Is constantly hounded by publishers
Each trying to outscore the other
Claiming to be the best in the business

Where does the newbie author go
Waiting to create a niche for self
Finds the publishing houses at loggerheads
And decides to give it all a rest!!

Writing a book is not everyone"s cup of tea
To this i"ve always agreed willingly
Here I was looking forward to a collaboration
Alas,i ended up at the receiving end of other"s frustration!!

Why don"t i get my own stuff published
Rather than being a part of the battle ensued
This way i will get my share of good night sleep
Keeping the publishers at arm"s length to upkeep!!

Sour Grapes

The hushed whispers were on
Ladies having a tete a tete
I know how she got the promotion
Must have offered herself in liasion!!

Offended by the bitter words
Years of hardships in vain
She hastened her footsteps
Deciding to approach her perpetator

Gathering every ounce of courage posessed,
She decided to lash out in outrage
You call yourself my friends,she lamented
Get out of my sight,before i lose my cool

Better to have a few genuine friends and well wishers
Than hoards of fairweather friends to parade around
I need positivity around me to motivate
For them,its a question of sour grapes!!

A poem dedicated to Adidev on his birthday

Adidev!!

Adidev kept me glued with his robust vitality
Child in his innocence,mature in his personality!!

The little genius reminded me of Einstein
I was sure,this kid was bound to shine
After capturing my heart with his endless chatters
The environment turned bright with genial laughter

Years flew by and Adi the superstar
Kept on adding laurels from afar
Be it his culiniary skills as a chef
Or a trip to the saloon to look his best!!

Climb the path to glory,if i may say
Tommorow is yours to conquer everyday!!
Stay blessed wherever you are
Let sky be the limit,rockstar!!!

Whispers in the Corridor

Whispers in the Corridor
Enthuse me endlessly
Shadows in the corner
Mesmerise me flawlessly

My outlook widens across the horizon
Approaching footsteps reem me dumfound
Instead of running amok wildly
I remain rooted to the ground

Pindrop silence finally greets me after a while
Managed to shoo away death barely across a mile
Front page headlines screamed loudly the very next day
A braveheart had managed to keep the serial killer
at bay!!

Fan

He heroworships the ground his idol walks on,
Stalks him from afar,
Far from the madding crowd
And ofcourse the beefy bodyguards

If only i can spot my man
I will feel as elated as i can
I know they pay a price of fame
Its not easy being a household name

As he"s gearing up to pose for a selfie
Only to realise everything has gone messy
Heroes and idols are only humans
Agony and ecstacy is what they reckon!!

My plans to have fan moments fawning
Are replaced with ones of me yawning
Better to give my warrior some space
Lest he disappears without a trace

Away from the shutterbugs,
Peaceful life awaits
Like a breath of fresh air
All in all they anticipate!!

Vacation

Holidays are moments to relax,to distress and chill,
To do everything as per will
Not only do they give a sense of thrill
Its as if time had always stood still!!

Whenever one reaches their favourite destination
Caution can be thrown to the winds during vacaction
Explore the hill top from dusk to dawn
Be a beach mermaid and talk of the town!!

Travelling gives immense pleasure
When one is away from day to day torture
Relive all the pleasant times
Be lost in the sweetness of wine!!

Working round the clock like a robot
Can bring boredom as an onslaught
Why not use sightseeing and adventure
As a gateway which works like stress buster!!

Why not make the most of a holiday getaway??
Keep work at an arm"s length anyway!!
Good times can never be postponed
Time and tide waits for no one!!

Dusshera

Dusshera signifies the victory of good over evil
The one who was killed was Ravan
The one who emerged victorious was Ram
Was Lord Ram really a saint and Ravana a sinner??

Arrogance,Ego,Ambition were in their bloom
Ravana,the learned warrior met with his doom
Lord Ram and Demon Ravana found a place
In Valmiki's epic Ramayana!!

Lord Rama made Sita undergo Agni Pariksha
The quientessial mama's boy quietly went into the woods
Lust,Ego,Ambition,Greed killed Ravana
Humbleness,Sacrifice and love saved Rama!!

No one is Ram in this day and age
Neither is their Ravana inside us
Chosing the right path is all that matters
Kill the demon inside,bring the saint outside

Celebrate the magic of Dusshera like no other
Bring cheer,happiness galore at your disposal

Nepotism

The torchbearer of nepotism was on a mission
Ensuring the success of the newbies
Seemed to be his obsession

The hatred ran deep,boycott was the word
It spread like wildfire,it struck a deep chord!!

Im not promoting the oft spoken expression
Nor am i supporting the cause!!
All im taking is a pause

Before crying foul,shouting from the rooftops
Think,contemplate and analyse
Wasnt nepotism omnipresent always
Just looking for a reason to be promoted

The children of doctors are mostly doctors
The progeny of businessmen,end up as entrepreneurs!!
Before shunning and shutting down nepotism
Think how it will honour the profession

Its bad to encourage those lacking in talent
Nothing wrong in motivating gifted abudance
Genes always do the talking
Ignore all you can,theres no escaping!!

Mind you its no childplay
Those emerging succesful are bound to stay!!

Flowers in the graveyard

Flowers in the graveyard
Gloryifying the dead
Amidst whispers and shadows
They remain to be heard!!

Signifying the presence of the souls
Who remained unknown alive
Expressing the age old adhage
Of paying a tribute or homage!!

The inaminate objects weave a magic
Of fragrance that defies any logic
The crocodile tears of the grief stricken
Aims to bring relief to the heartbroken!!

Reduced to ashes,they prove their worth
Ironically,hollow in their birth
All their lives craving to be in the headline
They become an obituary as a deadline!!

Weather blues

Windy,Ruffled,Muddy Rain
Casts a Magic Spell, Yet no Gain
Worrisome Weather it is Come- Hither
Thunder and Lightning,running helter skelter!!

The summer sun was at its peakest now
The brightness tanning everyone and how
The hidden clouds played peek a boo
Announced the shower of blessings achoo!!

Unpredictable it is,but true to the core
Forecasting how the day goes confuses us more
Basking in the sunshine is a thing of the past
Enjoy the beauty of monsoon till the drizzle lasts!!

Season change affects us all
After heat disappears,there"s rainfall
How green is my valley, enchanted,i say
The beauty and fragrance of flowers mesmerises me
today!!

The universe conspired to keep us glued
Leave us transfixed till we bid adieu
Umbrellas and raincoats ensure we remain confined!!
Summer exits,Monsoon enters,Can winter be far behind??

The Teacher

A friend,philosopher and guide
Always willing to lend a helping hand
Selfless to a fault,kind at heart
A teacher sets an example,by default!!

A humble and hardworking soul
Shapes the lives of umpteen
Carves and moulds them through inspiration
Even though battling their own perspiration!!

A teacher stands tall,like a leader for all
Strict yet wise,staunch and resilient
Lending a patient ear to listen
The sacrifices of a teacher can never be forgotten!!

I bow to thee,even though they don"t expect
The profession deserves immense respect
Our parents bring us into the world
But a teacher's contribution cannot be challenged!!

Junk food

Food for your thoughts really
As long as it appeases my belly
Let go of this trash if you may
Junk food is harmful for health they say!!

The taste aroma and flavour intoxicate
Its multilingual cuisine mix and match,why not
appreciate??
The way to our hearts is through the tummy
Sweet and savory,fried or roasted,its yummy!!

Keep on gorging on delicacies,relish all
Dont count the calories,polish it off
No substitute for cakes or burger
Let them go easy on your bladder

A trip to the doctor will be on the cards
Stick to a discliplined diet,my ward
Dont stop eating my friend,nor indulge in dieting
Make fitness a part of your regime unending!!

What"s really cooking as we contemplate
The smell emanating from the kitchen has been worth the
wait!!

Books

In this world of make believe
Make books your best friends
Flip through the pages
They are for all ages!!

As the great Francis Bacon said
Some books are to be tasted
Some to be swallowed
Others to be chewed and digested!!

Books come in all shapes and sizes
They cover a large range of topics
Be it for a specific class or endless mass
Reading is gender, age and religion no bar!!

Fiction, non fiction,heavy duty or light reading
Thriller, Horror, Satirical or Romance
They cast a spell on you, leave you in a trance
Keep you in splits or in a fantasy land

Whenever in best of spirits or down in the dumps
Look out for them as a saviour to share!!
Books never betray like friends can
Its time to visit the nearest book store again!!

Special Child

Children are always special
Irrespective of the traits they display
They wish to be loved, cared and nurutured
Not to be jibed at, chided or called absurd

Autistic, Dyslexic,slow learner and mentally challenged
Doesnt necessarily mean someone is deranged
 Empathy is the need of the hour
Not to make fun of them year after year

Anyone can be born with disabilities
Some endure them over time
Given enough support, motivation and guidance
Help create genuises on the line!!

There is an Albert Eienstein hidden in one
Another can be Mozart in the future
Asperger"s syndrome made Michael Angelo a sculptor
And Bill Gates, the richest!!

Spare a thought for the parents
There"s hidden suffering in their laughter
Love each child as a living being
Dont categorise as abnormal!!

Throw your arms wide in a bear hug
Dont form opinions or be judgemental
Reach out to kids with special needs
It will be a noble gesture indeed!!

Cassanova

The astrologer and palmist were clueless
The horoscope proved to be useless
All efforts went in vain
To find a prospective bride again and again

The cassanova was the talk of the town
He"s a player, refuses to be tied down
True to his image of Lord Krishna
He preferred to be surrounded by lots of gopiyan

Time flew by and the playboy sighed
Enough of sowing my wild oats, he cried
Let me find a partner now he recokned
I"m sure plenty of fish in the sea to beckon

Lure of the money tempted many damsels to be
his cinderalla
When he announced i"ll marry now Voila
Marriage plans further lead to his doom
The bride to be ran off with the best man of the groom!!

Left high and dry at the altar he cut a sorry figure
Waiting for him was a piece of letter
The runaway bride's words were crystal clear
Being a trophy wife is not for me, my dear!!!

India, My Motherland!!

I dream of an India where we stand united
Where the thirst for each other"s blood is missing
What people pine for is each other"s blessing
Not how much the other person is earning

India is free of chains
All lie under one roof irrespective of religion, caste,
creed and sex
Where the heart rules,money is secondary
We crave for love, not for money!!

The women of the nation are safe
Inside the womb as well as on the streets
The elderly dont die unattended
Counting days and night in their empty nest

The lure of the foreign land will die a natural death
If the desires of the worthy are met here step by step
Depression ought to be eradicated
Happiness galore, the mission planted!!

 I dream of an India where everyone stands equal in
the eyes of law

Truth prevails, the guilty gets no bail
The golden bird stands tall in its glory
This is how i want to write its story!!

Honeytrap

They met on facebook
Virtual strangers
Became lovers
It wasnt just an affair
They were spotted everywhere

Then the woman vanished overnight
Ghosting was she,he wondered with fright
How to survive those painless nights
He questioned himself with all his might

Suddenly the phone call arrived on a Wednesday
My life is in danger,Ive been asked to keep you at bay
Pay us up any day
Or else end up dead is all they say!!

Pining for the love of his life,his princess
Without hesitation he transferred all his riches
The pauper waited in vain for his beloved
Just to realise he"d been conned and shoved

I have the videos ready to be made viral
And have you ousted lock,stock and barrel
The threat rang large in his ears
He suddenly became a shadow of his former self,outgrew
the years!!

He acknowledged he"d lost his track
Fallen into a honey trap
Mission suicide was on his agenda

Fear of shame and humiliation, the reason behind the
propoganda
His family stood by him thick and thin
He got power to survive from within
He approached the police for help
Discovered he wasnt the only victimised jack

Thanking his stars,having learnt his lesson
He swore never to follow his instinct without any reason
Once bitten and twice shy
All he could do was stand and sigh!!!

Solitude

Far from the madding crowd
He lives a life of solitude
Free from the hustle bustle of this chaotic world
Which drives him insane time and again!!

Escapism is not his approach
He is driven by serenity
Peace and quite is all he needs
And a life of tranquility!!

Let me enjoy the greenery of nature
Be one with the environment to nurture
Free of pollution and outward artificiality
A life of genuinuity, harmony and solidarity!!

The nomad in him refuses to stop
The desire to travel remains atop
Aiming for spirituality at the onset
To quench the thirst of a wanderlust!!

Why i write

I write because Pen is mightier than the sword!!
An expression through words makes a mighty impression
Being the mouthpiece of others via your verses need
recognition
Conquering the concept of extraordinary courtesy the
power of imagination

Creativity is enhanced through the vocabulary fixation
Emotions captivated by the lenghty description
Isolation,loneliness,depression are replaced by a feeling of
elevation
Nostalgia,Euphoria mark the end of hysteria
Writing dons the mantel of a best friend by the end
of the era

No room for boredom in this world of illusion
Moments of mayhem witnessed in this art of sophistication
Reading between the lines is some sort of consolation
Embrace this glorious concept
After all the art and the artist need no introduction!!

The birthday girl

The birthday girl is forever grateful
A year added to her life
The spark and glory which never dies
Thanks,she says through tearful eyes!!

The wail marked the beginning of her arrival
The celebration the start of her survival
To stand tall,whatever surfaces
She withstood the b"day bumps with a smiling face!!

The journey had just begun,for heaven's sake
Why,hyper excited to taste the bite of my b'day cake
Childlike enthusiasm at display while opening the presents
Age doesnt wither the eagerness to escape spending a
single cent!!

Counting her blessings,she moves around like a modern
day cinderalla
To the loud and blaring music creating a lot of hoopla
Its my day she mutters to herself,let me have fun
For others its the end,for me the day has just begun!!!

Hypocrisy

The politician"s speech was over followed by a thunderous applause
Forever in news about his views regarding the upliftment of women
He was the toast of the town for his fight for a noble cause

The girl child has to be encouraged to study,
If the lady of the house is educated,its good for the entire family
Many schemes and scholarships have been introduced
To ensure the women of our nation are always on the move

What a man,we will definitely vote for him
Whispered the audience,held captive from within
We need such leaders for our country"s growth
To wipe off the patriarchal culture by its root!!

Reaching his house,the man completely ignored his daughter

Who rushed with her arms stretched to greet her father

Stared in contempt at his wife who had her face covered from head to toe

Asked her to get him whisky and polish his shoe

Yes,this was how the great man was living in his home

He,who worked for the emancipation of women all along

Its all for the votes my dear friend he said

When he made plans to kill another girl child in the womb,once again!!

Ode to a single mother

Give the baby up for adoption
Everyone said in unison
It was the result of just one night of passion
Will stand in the way of your glorification

No need for further specification
Even if the laws dont permit
Im not geared in for an abortion
At the expense of my own condition
And the single mom marched ahead with her decision!!

Sniggering and sniding remarks behind her back
Hurt her already bruised self,
Under the guise of sympathy and a helping hand
Many propositions came her way time and again!!

She fought the world with all her might
Brought up her bundle of joy on her own
Never letting him out of her sight
Fearing the worst was yet to come unknown

To her delight her sacrifice didnt go in vain
Her source of delight was now a robust young man
She thanked her stars for not falling prey
To vultures who thought she was an easy lay!!

The countless nights of love and devotion
Heaped rewards in the form of her son"s pleasant
dispostion
Who always stayed by her side,through thick and thin
When all deserted her citing fear from within!!

The martyr

Not a single eye remained dry
Nor was there a pin drop silence
When covered in the Indian tricolour
Distinguished trade mark of the body of the martyr

The bereaved widow found it tough to control her tears
While national honour of 21 cannon salute was bequeathed
upon her husband"s pyre!
You"re a brave woman,dont grieve,she consoled herself
Holding her infant clinging son
Bidding adieu to a stranger,he will never know

The mind went back to the countless sleepless nights she
had lain in anticipation
While her husband lay fighting in the border for the
nation
No reward of gallantry bequeathed for his sacrifice
Could compensate for the agony she would face in the
coming day and nights

The mother who had lost her son in the battlefield
Came forward to wipe the wet eyes
Look at the brighter side of the moments gone by
Both of us can work in unison,you and I !!!

A ray of hope marked the new beginning
The arrival of a camaraderie or family bonding
The former supported the latter
Ensured there will be no dearth of bread and butter!!!

Status Symbol

The middle aged man went on announcing to all and sundry
Literally shouting from the roof tops
My son is an NRI,he earns in dollars
My daughter is married to an NRI,she has a dream life!!

Years passed by,mega bucks being passed on to and fro,
Every year there was a visit from abroad
Laden with goodies and necessities galore
No amount of material comforts to care and spare
Could compensate for the lack of time to share!!

Two decades had passed,the yearly meet ups lessened and lessened
The old couple looked saddened as if approaching a
dead end!!
Money was no alternative for lack of emotions
Video calls no substitute for psychological stagnation

Suffering from an empty nest syndrome
They took shelter in an old age home
Miserable and alone,they looked for company,
Feeling all but buried and gone!!

Is it too late now,the couple whispered to each other?
To start afresh as if the years never went by,
We dont want luxuries to survive,
Just a few words of love and affection
Is all we need to thrive!!

The realisation struck but a wee bit late
Covid ensured the children reached just in time
The old couple breathed their last
Away from people they called 'Mine"!!!

The beggar

Bystanders laughed at his tattered attire
Mocking,jeering,sarcasm at its worst
Not a hair in place,dishevelled clothes
Yes the trademark of a door to door beggar

Window panes were tightly closed
Be it of houses or cars
Whenever the footsteps announced
The arrival of the beggar from afar

Shoo away you piece of filth,
The gentleman cursed underneath
Seeing you so early in morning
Has ruined my day for the evening

Reaching his very destination
Ironically he became a loser
A beggar can"t be a choser,he muttered
 Counting crisp notes left at his office counter!!

Who is on trial here,the giver or the receiver?
Both are,and we blame the person who has the stamp of a
beggar!!
He begs openly,the world begs under a guise
Receiving bribe underhand,then rejoice!!

Theres no shade of black or white
Grey is what matters
Next time you see a beggar approach
Dont shie away of him to reproach!!

Recluse

Far away from the madding crowd
He breathes in fresh air
No prying eyes can fathom
The mind relentlessly at work

Being labelled an introvert
He goes about doing the job at hand
Im answerable to nobody
The motto that guides him!!

The quest for something unique
Keeps haunting him from within
Thirst for knowledge is what ties him
To inner walls of the house daunting even!!

Neither is he an aimless nomad
In search of wanderlust
Nor is he a psychopath on a prowl
Staying awake on nights like an owl

Leave me alone he whispers into the darkness
Now a mere shadow of his former self
The delicate body collapses
Having shut the door of any horizon
Death awaits as the final destination!!!

Clickbait

Gossip sells like hot cake
With sugar and spice,prolong the bake
Rest assured,play it safe
Add a dash of Clickbait

Promise thrills,frills,go for the kill
Click on the link,pay a hefty bill
By the time the realisation strikes
Youve been duped,as if hypnotized

The headlines promise more than they can deliver
The reader ends up being the loser
Half baked knowledge is never an option
Still the moving fingers are a foregone conclusion

Better to be safe than sorry i feel
Its always been a mass appeal
As the moving fingers itch to press the button
Saying no,rise to the occasion!!
Or else lose every information!!

Its a trap laid to shred you off every penny
Money all gone,no sign of honey
Created a huge uproar galore
All was lost but for a public furore!!

Vendetta

Barbarism has no religion
Just an excuse to wreak havoc
Brutality at its worst
Sickening to the core
Emanating disgust

Innocents attacked and crucified
Slogans raise a hue and cry
There"s no turning back the clock
No time to reflect and sigh

Unabashadly and unapologetically
Vandalism has destroyed humanity
Fanatics gloat and celebrate
Mission accomplished for them

An inexplicable rage boils within
To see something so inhuman
Is this the goal we"ve set out to achieve
Killing,Destroying,Plundering,Lynching!!

I hang my head in shame and disbelief
Hoping this is just a world of make believe
Far from the madding crowd,i hope to achieve
Peace,Tranquility,Happiness and a Good Night sleep!!

Depression

Learn the art of expression,
Rather than fade into oblivion
Channelise your emotion
Lest it ends in depression

Seek help,reach out to family and peers
Its not something to hide but repair
It can save you from momentary despair
Ensure you receive comfort,care and share

Not to be ignored,nor to be sidelined in jest
It can come unannounced like a hornet"s nest
Be cautious,if you see signs and symptoms
Entirely eradicate it out of your system

Zeal to live can get you through this
Consult a counsellor if you find something amiss
Dont fear the society,what"re they going to do?
For them its always been a taboo

Remain in cheerful spirits,bursting with enthusiasm
You get one life to live,thats the justification
Be back on your feet and on your track soon
When hit by sadness,emptiness and gloom

Depression is not a disease,nor a pain
Helped by loved ones,alive and fighting again!!

Beyond Bhubaneshwar

As i bid goodbye to bhubaneshwar with a heavy heart,
Carrying a plethora of memories along,
Time flew past by without batting eyelids
The short and sweet flying visit had come to an end!!

Gripped by euphoria,plagued by nostalgia
I bid the beautiful people adieu
Purity of heart collaborated with genuinity of souls
The melancholic atmosphere juxtaposed with gravity of
laughter

Family gathered under one roof as a unit
The intoxicating aroma of food left me spellbound
Caught in the spur of the moment
As the past mingled with the present
Lost in our coffee table conversations
Our penchant for living life as its utmost conclusion!!!

Its not just about the picturesque atmosphere!!
That cast its spell with its sheer magic
But as they say the beauty lies in the eyes of the beholder
Its the people in their finery who make it the real
bhubaneswar!!

Aarav....The rockstar

I am a fan of Aarav the rockstar
Fell for him hook line and sinker
The moment i set my eyes on him
The playful banter he greeted me with
Brought to forefront the child that lay within!

Forever bustling with enthusiasm
His gimmicks keep me glued
The mischievious and twinkling eyes
Reveal his mysteriously alluring mood

In this world where shady crooks mark their omnipresence
Aarav is like a bundle of innocence
Far away from the angry glares
He teaches us how to care and share

Gurgles of laughter weave a magic around
The mind takes the form of a playground
Tiny feet running helter skelter
Capture your imagination like no other

The tiny tot leaves me spell bound
Hide and seek Peek a boo ensure there's a sound
Never a dull moment when we are homebound
Aarav ensures that he's always around

Greeting the little prince is a source of joy
On my return i go ahoy!! ahoy!!

(Aarav is my nephew, a toddler whom I met in
bhubaneshwar)

Ode to a father

He slogs day and night to keep the home fires burning
Sweating profusely although humming
Cradling his little princess or prince to sleep
Playing peek a boo unless they weep

A mother is always put on a pedestal
A father taken for granted like a provider
The role can never be surpassed
A Dad never goes on announcing his class

Hurting deeply and crying inside like a lost baby
It pains immensly bidding goodbye to his doll who
outgrew her nappies
A father is expected to be a man,not shed tears
Although he might be dying inside out of sheer fear

A father's selfless love can never be questioned
The shield he provides can never be vanquished
Its definitely a proud moment,nothing to complain
We are always remembered by our father's surname!!

Superstition

Was it really an apparition
A figment of my imagination
That cast a shadow of supersition
In my day to day presentation??

Vodoo,witchcraft, blackmagic all under fire
The black cat crosses the path
Life comes to a standstill,thats its power
Religious sacrifice and offerings dominate
Hypocrisy is at its worst

Getting married to a bamboo tree,dog or cat
Will ensure your daughter is free from any trap
What to say,if the priest himself is a snake
Making a fool of innocent devout who know whats at
stake

Milk overboils and suddenly there is a panic
Stones are suggested by any random tantrik
The crows and utensils announce the arrival of guests
Specialities prepared for our ancestors to impress

Even though the self proclaimed God Men are behind bars
A mad rush to greet them in respective cars
Struggle for power forces them to believe in this myth
To seek blessings of such shady conmen is a must

Why are we educated illiterates,i mutter out aloud
Dont put broken mirrors in the room,i hear someone shout!!

Summertime

Empty roads give a deserted look
Barren streets announce the arrival of summer
The scorching sun burns endlessely
The temperature is on a rise round the clock

Cooling effect required nonetheless
To quench the neverending thirst
Coconut Water,Lemon Soda and WateMelon juice act as saviours
Of vagabounds on a rampage

The mercurial effect hides the clouds behind
The Rain Gods elude us all the time
Dont run helter skelter
Enjoy the glorious summer!!

Hope

The rays of the sun enchant and captivate
Struck by glory forever we hallucinate
Alluring music plays a melody
Reminds me of a bohemian rhapsody

The morning heat is extremely alarming
The signs of rains have been extremely misleading
Blood,sweat,toil and tears creates a yawn
The show must go on from dusk to dawn

Life is no rollercoaster ride with a missed chance
Grab onto it with all your might this instance
Opportunity never knocks twice
Dont ignore it as if in a trance
To succeed one has to go the distance

The future that awaits you with all its might
Looks rosy,colourful and shining bright
One door closes,another opens randomly
Patience and determination are prequisites naturally!!

Fashion Show

Catwalk on the stage,models on a rampage
Layers of pancake on an otherwise wrinkled face
Lest the shutterbugs question what"s your age??

Cut throat competition greets the designers
Launching their own brand,announcing the label
Waiting with a bated breath,till the camera does the trick
Papparazis hound the stage undaunted
The who"s who are waiting to witness the showstopper

The hoopla hoo refuses to die down
Wardrobe malfunction is the talk of the town
Models take centrestage,the fashionnita on the lead
The front pages glare the next day,was she high on weed??

Glamour quotient is on a rise,the glitz of rave
parties,never dies
Its just a part and parcel of the game
Everything comes attached with the price of fame!!

Young and full of life,the red carpet comes alive
Old and gawdy,theres no way to survive
Yes,a dark life exposed nothing to amend
Distraught,fighting alone,meet a sad end!!

Narcissist

Gloating at self while staring at his reflection
He unabashadely proclaims himself to be a narcissist
Yes i"m obsessed with I,Me and Myself,sign of a self
confessed perfectionist!!

The mirror doesnt do justice to his image
In his eyes its just a vision beyond age
Where else can i get more mileage
Media knows nothing,he breaks into a rage

Pitfalls of a futile mind refuses to let sense prevail
Turning a cat and mouse game,something trivial to travail
A prisoner on the run evading law
A con man to the core is what i saw

This reward is nothing,my weight is worth in gold
Earn it,lest i end up getting old
Let people remember me as someone bold
Who lived life kingsize,duping people out in the cold!!

Reunion

Long lost friends meet to exchange pleasantries
Till a knock on the door breaks into her reverie
Was that a dream,just an illusion
A figment of my imagination??

No,its real,she pinches herself to feel
Champagne on the house adds to the zeal
Hustle bustle commotion all around
Ensures the escapist in her searches for fresh air

Bouts of laughter tear into the magic spell
The blazing music further adds to her agony
The time comes to a standstill
When the alarm bells mark a cacophony

Better not to attend such reunions
When i"ll end up searching for my companion
This is what she ends up with
And prefers fading herself into oblivion!!

Rendezvous

Hearts skipped a beat across crowded corridors
Silently the mouths hummed
"Your place or Mine"
Looking for a Rhythm Divine
I ended up sipping a glass of wine!!

Everything looked hunky dory until the morning sun rays
played truant
Hit by a Livin da vida Loca
Found self alone with an angry temperament!!

Dont read love into your One Night Stand
Lust never becomes love,youre not the only one,
understand!!
He ended up tearing his hair in a fit of rage
No place to go to,was kicked out of home in disgrace!!

How can i face anyone again
Never will i indulge ever in this game
Sad but true,Unless there"s pain there's no gain!!

Golddigger

They flock to the men like bees to honey
Hang on to them like their arm candy
Yes,they have this devil may care attitude
We"ve got the looks,so why not oh dude!!!

They flaunt their beach bods,while they suck the men dry
of their money
Proudly proclaiming their ownership on their partner's
every penny!!

Golddiggers can be spotted everywhere
Waiting to pounce on their prey unawares
Why"re we targetted,singled out,going by heresay
The trophy wives left alone,dont we have a say??

Be cautious lest you fall prey to golddiggers
The red flags visible in their come-hithers,
Easy succumbing to the charms of the floozies
Entrapment comes easily to the sugar babies!!

Never say you werent warned in advance,
Men themselves go announcing their bank balance
Deprived of their riches,taken to the cleaners
Struck by lightening,they cut a sorry figure!!

Rhythm of the Rain

Rains,where art thou??
No thunderstorms,no pre monsoon showers,
Clouds playing peek a boo
Hiding under the shrouded view!!

The scorching sun continues to bite and agonize
Drizzle,i wait with a bated breath for you to eulogize
To celebrate the arrival of drops enchanting us from dusk
to dawn
And wipe off those sweat glands enforcing us into a yawn!!

Miles and miles away theres no sign of pearlie rains
The farmers enduring heavy pain,yet no gains
I bow to thee raingods have some mercy
And shower their blessings on those thirsty
Eager to welcome the rhythm of the rain
And surrender to the madness which drives me insane!!

Netflix

Netflix, O netflix
You always leave me in a fix
What to watch,what not to
Is a moment of temporary bliss

The OTT platform has entered our domain like never
before
What could not be fathomed,say,a decade back is now
offered on a platter
Those raw and hidden talents unearthed and exposed
Which remained mere shadows or caricatures in a
blockbuster

Its goodbye to saas bahu endless sob sagas
And given us something to celebrate for a change
The movies and web series boast of an international
audience
And its proven that we offer more than mere dances
around the trees

As i remain glued to the idiot box with popcorn,nachos
and chips
I whisper to myself,youve taken me for a six,O
netflix,yes,Netflix!!

Kleptomaniac

I had no inkling whatsoever of what she was upto
Till i saw the remnants of missing toothpaste
I have no control at all over my actions,she replied
Im just a victim of circumstances

Atleast i owe up to my misdeeds,acknowledge my impulse
to steal
There are others who use it as an excuse
And act as if its a part of their appeal

Neither am i winona ryder,who was caught shoplifting,
Nor am i an ordinary mortal on the run like a beggar
Im just a human who goes by sheer instinct
To act according to their whims and fancies very much
distinct!!

Arent you all kleptomaniacs in a way
Dont you steal peoples heart
Deprive them of their sleep
Why target me alone then
When there are plenty who deceive??

Running short of answers,i decided to keep quiet ,
And,let the kleptomaniac wriggle out of the answer with
all her might!!

Morning Walk

What a sight to see in early morning hours
Animal conference on with a bang
Bulls whose horns might injure you
Waiting at the gate to welcome thou!!

Cows engaged in meet and greet
Totally lost to the world while grinding their teeth!!
The dog"s bark announces its entry
To make its presence felt and add to the reverie

Human safety should be the top most priority
Rather than denouncing it all to prove one's superiority
Thank the stars,managed to escape the clutches of
catastrophy
Inspite of hazards present in the form of human
anthropology!!

Heaved a sigh of relief,happy to breathe in the fresh air,
Tommorrow though will be another day of despair!!

(The poem wishes to draw attention of all to stray
dogs,bulls and cows,who are present in the
colonies,putting bystanders lives at risk!
People are actually requested to keep the chappatis or
whatever food item they wish to give them in a box or
separately,so as not to unnerve or inconvenience others.)

Modern Love

Long distance relationships rule the roost here
Public display of affection out in the open
But,within the four confinement of the house,strangers to each other

Celebrating holidays with their respective exes
Congratulating each other by instagram posts
Yes,the very same people who were washing dirty linen in public
Have now become the mouthpiece of each other"s new relationship!!

Pre nuptial agreements announcing the end of a marriage even before its beginning!!
A world where face times and texts rule the day
The human touch is missing but we are soulmates

Welcome to the world of modern love
Replace happily ever after with as long as it lasts!!
And the old school goers have the last laugh!!

The courier guy!!

Parcel...i heard a voice calling
The delivery man was standing there sweating in the sun!
Would you like a glass of water,i asked him??
No,ma"am have to rush to finish my quota of the day,was
his reply!!

Ding Dong,another doorbell rang just after i had closed it
The swiggy guy was present holding mouth watering
goodies of biryani by kilos
I looked through the keyhole
The incident of a woman being attacked
By the Pizza Delivery boy
Fresh in my head
Keep it outside,and leave went my reply

Tring tring,the guard of the appartment announced the
arrival of Amazon guy
Send him in i said! Kept my mask on
Be humane,i said to myself
Bhaiyya(Brother) take this,i said,ready
with a glass of lime water in my hand!!

Thanks,he said,people like you are rare to find
The smile and the reply certainly made my day!!
Beaming to myself,i said,will order something again!!

The IPL fever

The IPL continues to weave its magic year after year
A lot of moolah raked by the players who fill up their
pockets
To afford the glamourous,glitzy jet set lifestyle

High profilers get sold to the highest bidders at the
auction
Some are lucky,others remain unsold
Passions run high,performance on a strive

The lure of the coveted contract,
The power of the cherished mega bucks
Appeals to the charismatic players
When national duties come calling
Suddenly they are down with injuries!!

Who am i to complain,i say!!
Keep them coming and coming
Glory of the sixes,announce the arrival of the orange cap
Tumbling wickets signify the importance of the purple cap
The team huddle depicts a camarederie wherein East
meets West
And remain one big happy family!!

We remain entertained,neither is it a pain,nor a gain
Till this IPl exits just to begin again!!

Creativity

The aroma of food emanates the air,
The fragrance of freshly cooked delicacy fills up my
nostrils,
Similarly for a gardener blooming lillies and daffodils
Announce the arrival of spring

For Michael Angelo creativity lied in his sculpture
For Mozart in his symphony!

For Leonarda da Vinci and Picasso,they appeared in their
paintings
For the strongest music compositions
the artistes have their muse

For O Henry the writer,The last leaf remained his
masterpiece!!
And for Shelley,the sweetest songs revealed the saddest
thoughts

Creativity lies everywhere,be it the culinary skills of a chef
The magic show of a magician or even the rhythm of the
rains
The beauty especially lies in the eyes of the beholder
It leaves you enthralled and spell bound like music to ears!!

KK

Long before i became a fan of Kangana,the actor or
Emraan Hashmi the serial kisser
The soulful haunting voice which mesmerised me was of
the singer!!

Be it Tu hi Meri Shab hai or Dil Ibadat
Tadap Tadap or Soniye
KK had struck a deep chord with the audience
Which can't be broken by death!!

We lost a great talent to mismanagement
A young life cut short in no time
The music still lives on and remains immortalised
The legend that was KK can never be forgotten

The melodies cast a magic spell
And speak louder than words
Rest in Peace in a happy place
Shower love from heaven"s above!!

Dreams and Despair

Dreams which remain unfulfilled lead to despair,
Gloom sets in, depression and anxiety bound to appear
Every cloud has a silver lining
Tommorow comes in with a new beginning!!

Remain calm composed and work hard,
To ensure success is your reward
Put fear and stress at bay
Let worries and pessimism wash away!!

Be optimistic,be motivated
Patience and determination is the key here
The world will salute your feat
Once you've reached the pinnacle of peak!!

(This poem is for the students/professionals who are
disappointed after not reaching their desired goals)

Childhood

Gurgles of laughter ring in the air
Shrieks of delight echoing everywhere
What a lovely sight it is to see
Children running as if not a single care

Innocent minds at work
Dont play by the rule
For them its neither day nor night
Just a time to enjoy with all might

The playground resembles a stadium
The atmosphere vibrant with activity galore
The chirping of the birds adds to the glory
Making this one big happy story

I try to turn back the clock
Become a child myself
The world looks so beautiful now
Seen through the unbiased eyes of a bundle of joy!!

Harakari of the English language

Slangs and shortforms are in vogue
Performing post mortem of the english language
Just the other day i was greeted with TYOT
I scratched my hair in disarray,only to realise
It was Take your own time!!

Should i shout from the rooftops or fume silently in anger
What has the world come to
That even Happy Birthday is now HBD

Stay composed my dear,reassures my friend
For you,its the english language,
For us its the time which is money
If we go into deep explanations
Instead of Bill Gates,we will be William Shakespeare

Money talks,Rest is all a farce!!
AWTEW...and i rest my case...
What?????
All's Well that Ends Well!!!!

Who am I??

An unknown entity
An anonymous vagabond
A hidden figurine,
A lack lustre being!!
V for Vendetta or
V for Victory??
A nameless faceless soul,
Wanders from place to place,
In pursuit of happiness,
Which eludes her!!

Doppleganger!

The virus beckons, I'm your doppleganger!!
How is it practically possible??
We are humans, You are a virus!
Do a self introspection mate!!
We destroy nature, we massacre humans!
Rape, Murder, Rob, Crucify, Plunder,
Isn't that a major blunder!!
The roads are clean, the gardens green
Pin drop silence, barring the chirpy birds!!
Breath of fresh air, sans the polluted air
Revenge of Covid19, basking in between
When will this all end, I ask myself,
Wearing a mask, clenching my gloves! There's a huge
question mark??
It's here to stay my friend, as virus is in you!
Even if Corona leaves, the fear will be within,
Lone Crusader, Fight your battle,
Rise to the task like hercules,
Lest the virus has the last laugh!!

Accident

Chance encounters,
Fate bought them together,
So near, but yet so far,
Was it for real?
Or a figment of their imagination!
If we are destined to meet, we will!
With such assurances, he bid her goodbye!
Yes, they met but as corpses lying next to each other.
He died playing Samaritan to a child,
She lost her battle to cancer!
Cupid had the last laugh!
Man proposes, God disposes!!

Daydreaming

Clandestine meetings,
NOt an eyelid battered,
Drenched to the core,
She lay waiting for her Prince Charming!!
Viola, omnipresent he was
With his trademark umbrella,
Only to vanish in thin air
Was it a dream, she said to herself?
Once she woke up from a deep slumber!
The water did splash, but from a bucket,
Get up sleepyhead, mom said!!
Who's going to write the exam??

Emotions

Emotions running helter skelter,
Thoughts in a dissaray,
Unkempt hair, lost persona,
Just a face in the crowd!
She walked oozing with confidence,
Putting such thoughts to rest
Don't judge me by my looks,
I'm neither a book, nor its cover!
Yes, I'm a nomad, waiting to discover,
What lies underneath or it's all over?

#Me Too

She scoffed at the idea of giving dowry!

It's a crime, she said!!

She wasted his hard earned money shopping!

It's my right, she said!!

Treat my parents as yours she said!

Keep your parents at old age home, she said!!

Fair, homely and convent educated, you want a wife or maid, she said!

Tall, Dark and handsome with an eight figure salary will do she said!!

Men are creeps, it happened to me too, she said!

No plum roles, no marriage, let's take him to cleaners, she said!!

Domestic violence intolerable, she said!

Mentally harassing men acceptable she said!!

Male Chauvinism sucks, she said!

Fake feminism rules, she said!!

Go figure why, I said!

It's all a sham, I said!!